Tullio
Pericoli

Woody, Freud
and others

SAUL

Tullio Pericoli

Woody, Freud and others

Introduction by Georg Ramseger
Story by Antonio Tabucchi
Preface by Steven Heller

Prestel

Introduction by Georg Ramseger
translated from the German by David Britt

Story by Antonio Tabucchi
translated from the Italian by Caroline Bearnish

Cover: (front) Woody Allen (Plate 47)
(back) Sigmund Freud (Plate 16)
Frontispiece:
Self-Portrait, 1986
India ink and watercolor on handmade card
76 x 57 cm
(30 x 22½ in.)

Distributed in continental Europe and Japan by Prestel-Verlag, Verlegerdienst München GmbH & Co KG, Gutenbergstraße 1, D-8031 Gilching, Federal Republic of Germany.

Distributed in the USA and Canada by te Neues Publishing Company, 15 East 76th Street, New York, NY 10021, USA

Distributed in the United Kingdom, Ireland and all other countries by Thames & Hudson, Limited, 30–34 Bloomsbury Street, London WC1B 3QP, England

Color photographs by Jean-Marie Bottequin, Munich
Offset lithography by Karl Dörfel GmbH, Munich
Typeset by Max Vornehm, Munich
Printed by Peradruck Matthias KG, Gräfelfing near Munich
Bound by R. Oldenbourg, Munich
Printed in the Federal Republic of Germany
ISBN 3-7913-1028-3

Contents

Preface

Is caricature really dead in the United States? Once there were scores of periodicals offering sanctuary to renegade graphic critics and comedians whose gift it was to distort a visage, metamorphize a body, and thus strip an individual of his or her physical defenses for all the world to see. The best of these caricaturists – those who are also astute cartoonists – reveal certain truths about their subjects. But truth can be dangerous. Today the outlets for honest caricature are dwindling. With few exceptions acerbic caricature of the kind produced by the venerable masters of the savage pen (Honoré Daumier, Thomas Nast, Georg Grosz) is today rejected by editors and publishers who refuse to offend the sacred cows. And that, of course, says a lot about the future of the form. For certainly the most effective caricature will be offensive to someone.

The masters of contemporary American caricature are the same artists who began in the late 1950s, when the country was becoming aware of its nascent inequities, and also practiced in the late 1960s, as the Vietnam War was at its fiercest pitch. David Levine, Edward Sorel, and Jules Feiffer mercilessly ravaged the images of Presidents Johnson, Nixon, Ford, Carter, and Reagan, and like the seditious "Pear King" drawing by French satirist Charles Philipon in 1831, their caricatures became indelible totems of dissent. Another form – the apolitical kind – is exemplified by Al Hirshfeld, the undisputed grandfather of American caricature. Since the late 1920s his special brand of drawn-from-life caricature and graphic jest has documented the performing arts of this nation. Years ago Hirshfeld was one of many theatrical portraitists published in newspapers and magazines, today he stands alone. When he retires will this genre of caricature discontinue? When Levine, Sorel and Feiffer decide to pass their batons will there be others to receive them?

Each year the potential crop of native American caricaturists withers owing to the harsh climate and environment. Without a hospitable marketplace what is the use of even attempting to harvest. Many talented young artists therefore turn from caricature to more welcome and lucrative forms of cartoon and illustration. However, those deeply concerned with the extinction of caricature do attempt to stave the tide, and keep hope alive. After all, there is no dearth of subject matter or targets for America, and indeed the world is rife with folly too.

But where does hope ultimately spring from? I believe that monographs such as this offer young artists strength, just as Tullio Pericoli's distinctive work provides a model – perhaps even a direction.

Pericoli is a caricaturist/cartoonist whose roots are in the European tradition – an approach to graphic commentary that eschews the simplistic idea or slapstick gag for personal statement using allusion, metaphor or allegory. Pericoli's drawings are multileveled explorations of form and content. The form is a beaux arts fascination with draftsmanship. The content is political, social, and cultural, though decidedly contemporary in terms of color palette and linear execution, these drawings are neither modern, because complexity is preferred over economy, nor moderne, because though he has style, he is not a stylist. Pericoli does not mimic fashion but is responsive to each specific idea. And his ideas are not regurgitations of the venerable past, but seductive interpretations with topical implications.

With information today being transmitted instantly through fiber optics the visual world is at our fingertips. This has given rise to the argument that the graphic artist as a recorder of life has become unnecessary. If true (and I suspect it is becoming more so), then *interpretation* based on moral and ethical value is what is expected of the contemporary caricaturist. In this book Pericoli poignantly interprets man's relationship to the environment even in his most lighthearted work.

Pericoli's primary fascination with literature is a humanistic pleasure. By environmentalizing the heroes of literature (and culture) he weaves their familiar faces into patchworks of image and icon. If one theme recurs in Pericoli's œuvre – perhaps from some personal history – it is the depiction of the hero as child. Through distortion and exaggeration his heroes become curiously smaller than life. Pericoli visually transforms a dewy eyed Mar-
Plate 20 cel Proust (1987) into the youth described in his
Plate 14 prose. He makes Robert Louis Stevenson (1986) one with the fantasy world he so brilliantly
Plate 6 created. And Ernest Hemingway (1986) innocently dreams the little boy dream of greatness and danger.

Caricature, whether political, social or cultural, invariably harnesses the great power of humor (whether acerbic or benign) to pump the heart and inform the mind. Pericoli is funny in form and content. His line is comedic, his ideas ironic. He uses color in the same way a comedian who does impersonations might use gesture to enhance the role he is playing. Pericoli's soothing colors not only attract viewer attention, they highlight the persona of his subjects. Freud's darkish complexion, Sartre's reddish nose, Foucault's amberish eye all subtly add truth to the humor.

Is caricature in the United States dead? The obituary has yet to be written. Perhaps Pericoli's work will encourage the grim reapers, also known as editors and publishers, to give graphic humor a reprieve. This book certainly proves that smart caricature, though rare these days, is always welcome.

Steven Heller

Fig. 1
Street, 1981
India ink and watercolor
on handmade card
38 x 57 cm (15 x 22.4 in.)

Who is Tullio Pericoli?

One thing is certain: in the history of European caricature, the English contribution is an outstanding one. The miracle of the eighteenth century, unparalleled elsewhere, still holds its fascination to this day. Four stars of the first magnitude in the firmament of satire – Hogarth, Rowlandson, Cruikshank, and Gillray – surrounded by a crowd of lesser luminaries, Reynolds, Bunbury, Woodward, represent an accumulation of satirical and critical talent that had no rival anywhere in Europe.

It was not to be expected that the nineteenth century would repeat this luxuriant crop of venomous talent. Not that satire had become extinct, by any means: but the likes of Heath, Leech, Tenniel, and their fellows were a milder breed than their fathers and grandfathers. This state of affairs lasted into the age of *Punch*, which began publication in 1841, three years after the accession of Queen Victoria, and set the tone, as it were, for the work that was done in graphic satire both in London and in the provinces. And a great deal was done, although none of it had that ultimate barbed quality, the ability to draw blood. The tradition survived in the shape of a critical insight into humankind and its weaknesses, though no longer into its nastiness and its perversity.

Not until modern times was there another decisive shift. A Max Beerbohm (1872–1956), a David Low (1891–1963), dipped their pens in vitriol once more. And if we think of the present day, with Ronald Searle (born 1920) or Ralph Steadman (born 1936), we can rest assured that the old hatred for a hateful world is still alive and can once more be conveyed, even in the "merry old England" that no longer wants to be quite so "old" and therefore can no longer be quite so "merry."

We have engaged in this brief survey in order to account to some extent for the fact that a country that has produced, and still produces to this day, such a wealth of satirical art – and a country whose very position is an insular one – feels no particular need to interest itself, say, in Continental caricature. Curiosity as to what happens, "over there," when the human creature is pinned down in the artist's X-ray viewfinder, is not particularly highly developed. And yet things are happening in Europe that deserve to arouse much more than a fleeting interest in the English-speaking world.

We accordingly take great pleasure in introducing the work of the Italian, Tullio Pericoli. His cosmopolitanism is unmatched. Pericoli's range, in his portrait caricatures, is not confined to Continental Europe: figures from English culture are as familiar to him as those from the country that has given us the *New Yorker*, Thurber, Steinberg, and David Levine. We believe that Europe and America will find much to celebrate in their first encounter with this extraordinary man.

The man whose works are shown in this book is called Tullio Pericoli. He was born in 1936 and lives and works in Milan. He is what is known as an original genius; not the sort of person you meet every day. The fact that it has taken as long as it has for this book to be published, and for museums outside Italy to show this artist's work, is one of the unaccountable vagaries of international cultural life, an organism whose ramifications leave many curious gaps.

Let us take a look at Tullio Pericoli's present status. Since 1984 he has worked as a political caricaturist and social satirist for the daily newspaper, *La Repubblica* (510,000 copies daily), and from 1976 through 1987 he worked in the same capacity for the weekly news magazine, *L'Espresso*. Since 1985 his work has also appeared in the literary monthly, *L'Indice*. This last-named journal had the idea of asking him for a regular series of portrait drawings of personalities in cultural life in all periods. The field was not an unfamiliar one to him: he had always interested himself in the faces of writers, painters, scientists, movie people – the face of "Culture," as it is represented by individuals. And now this interest developed into a new professional activity, to set alongside all those in which he was already engaged.

The diversity of his activities – as political satirist, social critic, illustrator, advertising artist, pure painter, mural artist, television designer – remains bewildering. He works on all these, alone in his Milan studio – and on sculptures in plaster and glue. He is a fanatically hard worker, but not a fanatic; a moralist, but not a Savonarola; a virtuoso, both in form and color, but never a slave to his own technical facility.

The main focus in the present book is on the caricature as portrait, divorced from national circumstances and universally valid; the spotlight will also be turned on some of Pericoli's other activities. This book is not intended as a monograph but as a selective review of his work: as such, it is the most important since 1985, when he started to work for *L'Indice*.

We do not believe that an artist who adopts a critical posture can ever be a great lover of the human race. He may have his likes and his preferences; but his inborn attitude must be one of detachment. There is one drawing of Pericoli's
Plate 4 that tells us a great deal: twenty-five heads, five times five, of recognizable contemporaries, each assigned to one of the letters, A–Z. The alphabet is constant, but the heads are varied in their attitudes. James Joyce chews on a U; Woody Allen, appalled, spits out a Z; Virginia Woolf holds the dot of an I between her lips like a cherry, while the body of the letter floats free; Bettino Craxi chokes on an O. No attempt is made to identify the individuals concerned: this is an elevated, rarefied view.

The patrician artist sitting in judgement on the world at large? It is a thought that cannot be ruled
Plate 5 out. The image of Italo Calvino – Pericoli's friend, and in this case his surrogate – gives the game away: high above the world, Calvino sits enthroned, narrow-lipped, with scorn playing about his mouth and eyes.

Fig. 2
Study for *Virginia Woolf*, 1987
Pencil on paper
35 x 28 cm (13.8 x 11 in.)

Fig. 3
Study for *Virginia Woolf*, 1987
Pencil on paper
25 x 18 cm (9.8 x 7.1 in.)

Let us begin this survey with a piece of invention that is unusually cunning, even for our guileful artist. *Plate 2* Everyone knows who David Levine is: he is the American artist whose portrait caricatures cover the same range of subject matter as those of Pericoli. Levine is the only artist who bears comparison with Pericoli, either for intuitive power or for incisiveness. By contrast, however, Levine is purely a master of monochrome, and he is extremely sparing in his use of accessories. An older man by ten years (born 1926), he has been famous for longer. Pericoli gives us a portrait of him that is also a tribute. Full-bodied, full of bonhomie, Levine cradles New York in his arms, and his people look out of the windows: Colette, Monroe, Freud, Keaton, Picasso, Sartre, and others. The postage-stamp format does nothing to impair the quality of a salute that spans an ocean. Pericoli appreciates Levine at his true worth. The two men are equally acute in their insights: what separates them is the element of stagecraft that gives the Italian the edge: the delight in play-acting, the theatricality, that provide him with a narrative and imaginative bonus.

Much the same creatures perform for both artists (the American has more Americans, the Italian more Italians). The criterion of "international reputation" is the same for both; although I have my doubts – and, again, this applies to both – as to where a just concern with fame ends and mere name-dropping begins. Be that as it may: for Levine the head is the focus of his efforts, and the body and the setting are mere accessories. His *Plate 6* Ernest Hemingway, for example, is no more than a hugely grinning giant skull, looming above the vestigial attributes of a body, a typewriter, and a few sheets of paper. Pericoli, on the other hand, stages a scene. He puts his attribute, a fierce, pouncing lion, into the center of the picture, and relegates the hunched, cloth-capped figure of his protagonist to the lower left-hand corner. If we start to suspect that the lion is really a toy, then we are probably on the right lines: no compliment to Hemingway is intended.

Both artists have their own versions of Kafka.

Fig. 4
Study for *Vladimir Horowitz*, 1986
Pencil on paper
35 x 28 cm (13.8 x 11 in.)

Fig. 5
Study for *Vladimir Horowitz*, 1986
India ink and pastel on paper
28 x 35 cm (11 x 13.8 in.)

Levine's has a long, narrow, emaciated head with
outsize, bat-like ears, floating above a diminutive
desk; the hands are insect claws, wielding a pen,
Plate 8 and below are blank pages. Pericoli's Kafka is a
full-length, Gothic-looking figure in a sorcerer's
mantle, towering above an assortment of diminutive framed photographs: Kafka as a baby, as a boy,
as a youth, as a man. Beset by himself, he finds no
way out. That is how Pericoli sees it.

Pericoli finds another version of self-absorption
Plate 11 in his Dostoevsky, which incorporates a crazy pictorial idea. Dostoevsky opens a door, and it is
simultaneously opened by another Dostoevsky
who stands behind it: a quotation from Duchamp.
Such games have their lighter side: Pericoli's
delight in detail is infectious. He places his friend,
Plate 12 Eugenio Montale, who has the head of a Roman
senator, in front of one of those old-fashioned type-
cases that people hang on the wall and fill with
meaning by placing an assortment of bric-à-brac
in the compartments. Pericoli adorns his type-case
with lemons, yarn, ladybugs, spiders, sheet music,
salamanders, a kiwi, photographs – all of which,
for all we know, may mean something to Montale,
novelist and Nobel laureate. To us, the effect is that
of a succession of impertinent ideas, a prank, such
as Pericoli delights in.

Plate 14 His paraphrase on Robert Louis Stevenson, on
the other hand, is a piece of pictorial grand opera.
Beneath a sky full of wildly billowing clouds, seven
schooners sail in search of the treasure island that
must be somewhere in a grotesque, luxuriant, fire-
spewing archipelago. From the midst of all this tur-
moil there emerges a narrow, aristocratic face and
a hand to match, wielding a grandly curving quill.
Stevenson was a sick man all his life; it is all there
in Pericoli's drawing.

Plate 17 He is a Rastelli of the pen. Look at his Einstein,
cycling wildly out of control with fruit, vegetables,
Plate 18 formulae, and a flapping violin; or at his Sartre,
with toppling sugar-bowl and papers a-scatter.
Plate 9 Look, especially, at his Joyce: the whole body a
single mysterious contortion, everything unnatu-
rally dislocated and entwined, as he painfully
reads with enfeebled eyes that have long needed a

Fig. 6
Appointment, 1986
India ink and watercolor on handmade card
38 x 28.5 cm (15 x 11.2 in.)

Fig. 7
Official Ceremony, 1983
India ink and watercolor on handmade card
38 x 28.5 cm (15 x 11.2 in.)

magnifying glass as well as spectacles. The bulging forehead, the pursed mouth – but alongside all this ugliness there is much elegance: the shoes, the coat, the vest, the bow, and the exquisite little cane. Rapt in contemplation, this lost lord of language remains, for Pericoli, in a category all his own. There is a reason for the portrait of Shakespeare, below: Shakespeare & Company, of Paris, were Joyce's first publishers.

Pericoli speaks with many tongues. And what he says is not for all ears. He likes to pose riddles, and many of his graphic ideas seem to have found their way into his mind by devious, pixilated routes before undergoing their metamorphosis into images. His riddles have a charm that is particular to them. There is the optical stimulus – so much to explore – and there is also a second form of curiosity: what is it all about? How much can actually be deciphered is quite another question.

Fig. 1 A typical Pericoli problem picture is *Street*: a blowzy female who lifts her skirts behind and shows us her bloomers. Street, as in streetwalker? Is that what it means? Her ample posterior is decked with a mixed assortment of images: Woody Allen (one of Pericoli's "saints"); the Mona Lisa; a clown; a ballerina; Verdi; Carmelo Bene, the *enfant terrible* of the Italian theater; a sheet of music. The lady is also hung about with a television, a tennis racket, and a mandolin. In her clawlike fingers she holds a tennis ball, and between her thighs she grips two or three books. Are these the landmarks in a life of which we know nothing? We can never know. But those who lurk beneath this woman's skirts are definitely not the artist's enemies.

This kind of hide-and-seek can be a pleasurable business, as when for example Pericoli shows his *Frontispiece* hand by giving us a self-portrait. This enshrines a multitude of things that one would like to know about this many-faceted artist. A melancholic looks out at us, sitting up in bed in the early morning. He has just put on his glasses, and he can see that the world has not improved. Red sky at morning, and looming clouds, promise no good. What he sees is the fate that lies in store for him: brushes and pens in their pots; paint boxes and tubes; ink

Fig. 8
The Days of the P38, 1986
(Cover for retrospective issue of *La Repubblica* on the year 1977)
India ink and watercolor on handmade card
38 x 28.5 cm (15 x 11.2 in.)

bottles and boxes of pastels; containers of all kinds; a palette; a Colombian sculpture; a rose in a little vase; a lady's shoe in a teacup; a man's boot; a bellows. He has stowed books and rolls of paper under the bed.

The books and the pictures allude to his ancestors: Dürer with his "Instruction in Perspective," Bruegel with his *Tower of Babel*, Rembrandt and Little Nemo, Robinson and Klee and Saul Steinberg. And the telephone, and an airline ticket to New York: the New York of Woody Allen, Steinberg, Levine? Sooner or later, he is going to get out of bed and add another day to his life; but not just yet. The dance on his bedroom floor is still in full swing: steel nibs, pencil stubs, paint tubes, letters of the alphabet, and odds and ends: a ballet of numbers and signs.

The detail-obsessed, prodigal creator shown in the self-portrait is not all there is to Pericoli. There also exists a quite different Pericoli, for whom caricature becomes monumental, a vision stripped of all extraneous elements. The massive head of a
Plate 25 thinker, like Benedetto Croce, conveyed with pas-
Plate 26 sion; Orson Welles as an Asiatic despot, diabolically composed: one grim countenance to form the massive body and above it a tiny head of Welles
Plate 23 with the features of a bloodstained tyrant. Günter Grass is another: a Genghis Khan in half-moon glasses. Looking at these two images, one cannot rid oneself of the thought that, for all the sharp penetration of his eye, our cocky Italian artist has not taken these Mongol potentates – from Kenosha, Wis., and Danzig respectively – entirely seriously.

Eyes are important for Pericoli. Most of his figures look straight out at us; although a few look askance, a device used with bold impudence in the
Plate 28 portrait of De Chirico, where the head rears up and we glimpse a pin-sized pupil. There are excep-
Plate 29 tions. Virginia Woolf has no eyes for us at all; Boris
Plates 30, 31 Pasternak's gaze is far away; Peter Handke squints past us, eyes peevishly narrowed.

One of the most striking and moving portraits
Plate 32 of all is that of the blind Jorge Luis Borges. A tired old man sits slumped against the gold nib of a

Fig. 9
Beniamino Placido: "It's like Rimini. You have to be German to get a hotel room."
From the series "Saturday Night at Fulvia's," April, 1983

gigantic fountain pen, like a beggar under a street lamp. His eyes are dead; he seems to see through his preternaturally wide nostrils. He scents the world that he can no longer see. The great man in all his weakness: an idea for which Pericoli has found a form that no one who sees it will forget. Caricature, for him, is not a way of belittling people. True, he sees through the mask to the real face; but he robs no one of his or her dignity. Of course, as a native of the Mediterranean world, he sees dignity as inseparable from a trace of self-dramatization, which it is permissible to smile at.

Pericoli the day-to-day political observer is something quite different. Here his temperament becomes passionate. His malice blossoms. The background loses some of its importance. The artist's hand reaches out, grips its victims – politicians or Princes of the Church – and wrings them dry: men like Andreotti, Berlinguer, Craxi, Nenni, Pertini. When he tackles his subjects in black and *Fig. 10* white, as a single image or in a strip, the pen becomes a hammer. He goes straight to the point and pulls no punches. This does not mean that he stops being funny: quite the contrary. Seriousness, for Pericoli, has nothing to do with earnestness. Together with his scriptwriter and friend, Emanuele Pirella – they have been in business together for years – he constantly comes up with *Fig. 11* cherishable miniatures like the Craxi cartoon that shows the Italian Socialist leader taking a dip and sighing: "I need to take a leak, but I don't want to alienate the Green Party."

His impersonal political work, which is in color, often transcends its narrow limitations of place *Fig. 8* and time. A handgun, towering above a typical Italian piazza with its houses and tiny human figures, points its accursed barrel into the wide, peaceful landscape: nothing has ever brought the meaning of terrorism so forcefully home to me as this image, *The Days of the P38*.

Pericoli takes a no less critical view of the State in which he lives his own life. There is the good citizen, joyfully unbuttoning his shirt to be rubber- *Fig. 6* stamped. *Appointment* is the title. The same citizen looks less enthusiastic in the companion piece, in

Fig. 10 John Paul II: "I am handsome. I am tall. I am strong. I am not the representative of Christ. I am the direct representative of God!" From the series "Palace Chronicle," *L'Espresso*, October 14, 1979

Fig. 11 Bettino Craxi: "I need to take a leak, but I don't want to alienate the Green Party." From the series "Palace Chronicle," *L'Espresso*, August 30, 1987

Fig. 12
Portrait of R., illustration for *Robinson Crusoe*, Olivetti, Milan, 1984
India ink and watercolor on handmade card
57 x 76 cm (22.4 x 30 in.)

which he is made to bend down and hoist his bare backside into the air. On it, another stamp is about to descend; only the stamp and the hand that holds
Fig. 7 it are seen. *Official Ceremony*, says Pericoli.

The artist is from northern Italy; he was born near Ascoli Piceno, in the Marches, a city which bears the name of a tribe that lived there in ancient times. Ascoli people are characterized as "descendants of those witty, sharp-tongued, intrepid Piceni of whom even the Romans were afraid." Now we know why Pericoli is so fond of tangling with those in power in Rome.

One part of his social criticism appears – once more in concert with Emanuele Pirella – in a cartoon strip whose protagonist is a lady called Ful-
Fig. 9 via, a garrulous representative of Milan's chic culturati, with every new fashion on the tip of her tongue. These are black and white drawings in a deliberately simplified style. The comic strip

Facing page:

Fig. 13
Study for *Igor Stravinsky*, 1986
Pencil on paper
35 x 28 cm (13.8 x 11 in.)

Fig. 14
Study for *Igor Stravinsky*, 1986
Pencil on paper
35 x 28 cm (13.8 x 11 in.)

Fig. 15
Study for *Igor Stravinsky*, 1986
Pencil on paper
35 x 28 cm (13.8 x 11 in.)

demands a lapidary economy with words. At one time, the new German cinema was in vogue in Milan: Fulvia goes into such ecstasies at every German name that her interlocutor – the Milan journalist, Beniamino Placido – wryly remarks: "It's like Rimini. You have to be German to get a hotel room."

Such is the wealth of material that this artist produces that we cannot discuss him with anything like the completeness that we would like. He had the good fortune to be commissioned to illustrate a book of his own choice to be sent out as Olivetti's corporate new-year gift for 1984. He chose Daniel Defoe's *Robinson Crusoe*. With a volcanic imagination and an almost manic appetite for detail, he set to work and invented the landscapes and seascapes that he needed, the island rising out of the water, the vegetation on the earth, the life in the sky above it, the beasts, the shifts in the weather, the man and his tools. Crusoe, to him, is *Homo faber* personified: a hulking fellow, a face somewhere between Darwin and Van Gogh. A man cast back on his own resources, who holds his own in a world that is unfriendly if not downright hostile: truculent, inventive, wily. Pericoli draws and paints human history as the invention of tools. The tool alone makes it possible for man to face up to Nature.

The black cloth binding of the Olivetti book bears a glued on card, 7.2 x 11.5 cm (2.8 x 4.5 in.), on which, above a reclining Crusoe, more than forty implements are shown, like illustrations in a mail-order catalogue: from an ax to a fish-hook, from tongs of all kinds to saws of every type, plus spyglass and inkstand, compass and dividers, pistol, musket, and saber. Pericoli is no Romantic but a visionary with both feet firmly planted in a mean world. His Robinson Crusoe material filled a one-man show in Milan in 1985, and a catalogue was published with 65 illustrations: "Drawings for Robinson, Landscapes and Figures." *Fig. 12*

Pericoli draws Crusoe's tools with meticulous precision, and the next instant he simplifies in a childlike scrawl, before revealing himself as a virtuoso whose every routine on the high-wire of line

Fig. 16
Thomas Mann, 1986. Pencil on paper, 35 x 28 cm
(13.8 x 11 in.)

drawing comes off with total naturalness. In the texture of his forms, he underlays the color with a delicate web of long drawn-out lines, cross-hatchings, and comma-like hooks. The portrait of Plate 33 Musil, for example, gives some idea of the range of Plate 45 this technique, or Buñuel.

In the beginning, for Pericoli, was the face. Look Fig. 16 at the pencil sketch of Thomas Mann, as gaunt and haggard as we have ever seen him. Pericoli sees Mann as a sufferer – which, among other things, he certainly was – and lays hold of the face with a roaring richness of lines in all possible variations, so that he burns this sadness indelibly into our minds. Pitilessness is not far away.

Pericoli is inseparable from his mastery of outline. His pencil studies confirm that line is always his point of departure. Take the process that Figs. 2, 3 emerges from the preliminary drawings of Virginia Figs. 4, 5 Woolf, of Vladimir Horowitz at the piano, and of Figs. 13–15 Igor Stravinsky: first the outline, then the detailed drawing, and last of all the color. However, that color is then sometimes driven home with such devastating logic as to make one forget the outline. Draftsmanship disappears; painting triumphs. The surface action retreats from downstage center: space is created, and used.

A revealing example of such a process of spatial development is the completed likeness of the Plate 37 French Structuralist philosopher, Michel Fou- Fig. 17 cault. In the foreground is the germ of the image, which is already present in the preliminary drawing: the bold bald head, a pupil swerving to the outermost corner of the eye. Behind this there emerges a room in which Foucault stands in front of an easel. His head, however, is subsumed into a drawing pinned to the far wall, which thus sets up a third plane. In that wall there is an open door, and a third – or rather a fourth – space is created. This space is a staircase, and so it ultimately opens up an endless space: one that is also endless in time. The whole background of the picture playfully quotes from Velázquez's *Las meninas* (1656), on which Foucault once wrote an essay.

Pericoli's use of color admits of no separation between drawing and color. He himself says of his own works: "I no longer know whether to call them drawings or paintings, and I don't really care any more." The preliminary drawings for his James Joyce tell only of the encounter with the face Fig. p. 144 and its immediate setting: the bow tie, the shoulders, the hand. The pictorial image is still a long Plate 9 way away: first comes the brown wall of books and then the infernal red of the jacket. The Handke is a Fig. 18 variation in black against a pale, towering sky; for Plate 31 Primo Levi, a light red supervenes against a soft, Plate 36 gray void.

The color is always effective, but – paradoxically enough – markedly restrained. In all modesty, so to speak, Pericoli risks some bold combinations while tending to leave the backgrounds comparatively nondescript so that any color, even a pale or

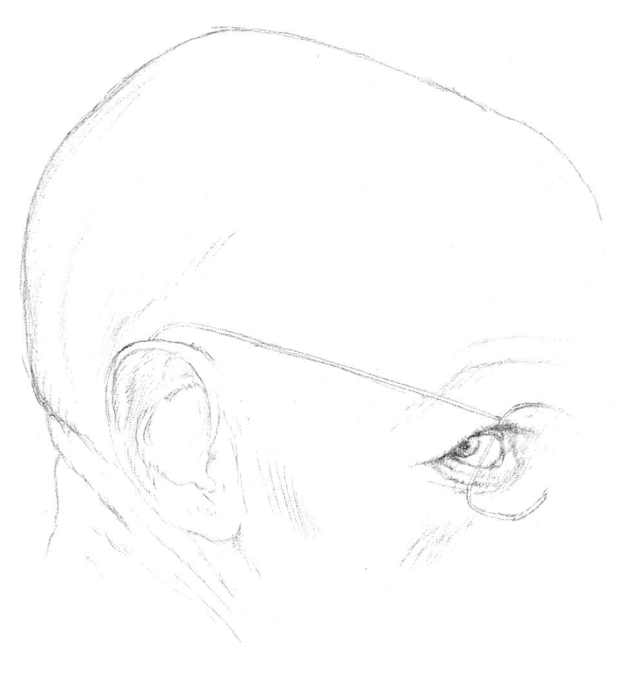

Fig. 17
Study for *Michel Foucault*, 1987
Pencil on paper
35 x 28 cm (13.8 x 11 in.)

subdued one, stands out effectively; especially when the painter – calculatedly – makes bright colors flash out of gray, ocher, pale violet, or thin yellow: a red-spotted necktie, a red-striped bow, a red rose, a fiery nose, a rich yellow nose, a blue scarf, a blue skirt, a white face.

These shots of bright color occur in specific details: in ties, shawls, hair, smoke, clouds, drapes; in all that blows, flutters, flies, wags, undulates. A dead calm would be unwelcome: there must be a gentle breath of wind at the very least. A stiff breeze is ideal. The billowing garments worn by his figures point to another of this painter-draftman's predilections: his flair for clothing in general. He never tires of it, even when he has a subject – an artist or a writer – who is an extremely sloppy dresser. His joy in clothes is transformed into a passion when it comes to shoes. The foot-
Plates 9, 42 wear of a Joyce, or of the man in *Flying Leaves*, or of
Plate 53 the architect in *Piazza del Duomo, Milan*, or of
Plates 32, 54 Borges, or of the dreamer in *Beneath the Stars* – all this is the best Italian workmanship. But he also dwells lovingly on the clumsier footwear of a Sartre or an Allen.

Beneath the Stars shows a completely different Pericoli. If we have hitherto been dealing with a man who sees faces, we now encounter the man
Plate 54 who sees visions. The universe is depicted as two separate hemispheres, the upper holding the firmament, the other representing our earth, on which a man lies dreaming: gazing into the
Plate 55 heavens. An alternative construction sees the universe as two cones, joined point to point, with the firmament in the upper cone and the terrestrial world in the lower; a figure contemplates them deep in thought, with dividers in his hand. Is this God as Architect, beginning to tire of the earth and the universe that we take for granted? There are other possibilities: the Earth as a cube, with very little room to spare for the blue of the sky; or as a thick rectangular plate, on which a tiny man stands holding up another rectangular plate which is the sky. Of course, all this manifests a deep disquiet with the world as we know it: a longing to escape from an inner confinement. And all this is to be taken entirely literally: the universe a globe which man (with tie fluttering) bursts through. I do not know whether Pericoli is suggesting something like the "Faustian" element in man, or whether he regards all such heroic endeavors with a pitying smile; his little men look puny, as they bear the weight of the skies or strive to break out into the Cosmos beyond the Cosmos.

There are surreal elements in all the ramifications of Pericoli's art. But one important side of it in particular – the one that we have just been discussing – belongs entirely within the realm of fantastic painting. Here, titles start to become deceptive. That "divine" cone-engineer was once entitled *The Melancholy of the Architect*: a clear insight into the vanity of human aspirations. But this was too direct for Pericoli. With a new title, *Composition*, *Plate 55*

Fig. 18
Study for *Peter Handke*, 1987
Pencil on paper
35 x 28 cm (13.8 x 11 in.)

Plate 56 Fig. 19

he transferred the image into a vague realm of total unreality. *The Big A* has nothing to rely on but its own capital weight as the first letter of the alphabet – by contrast, for example, with an image and a title like *The Big Ear*, where the indictment of our noisy civilization is made abundantly plain. As a pictorial idea, this is as frightening as it is brilliantly crude.

Realism is not prized. His mountains are arrangements of sugarloafs or B-cups; his clouds are surges of ganglia or guts; but they are mountains or clouds, for all that, and never for one instant could they be mistaken for anything else.

There is no longer any defining the point of departure, or the destination, of Pericoli's practice of art. We know that, right at the start, Klee and Steinberg were in there somewhere. But all that is over, now. He is now entirely his own man. He is impossible to pin down, and he very seldom gives anything away.

Something that Umberto Eco has written about the island world of Pericoli's *Robinson Crusoe* might equally well stand for the artist's entire work: "The things that Pericoli brings together come from far and wide: from Van Gogh, from Japanese painting, from the plates in eighteenth-century instructional works; from catalogues and decors of many different periods."

In an essay entitled "I on me," Pericoli himself once wrote: "Something shifts; a ray of light, and perhaps that is why I have sometimes alluded to Turner; an unveiling, and perhaps that is why I sometimes allude to Steinberg; a vibration beneath the skin, and perhaps that is why I sometimes allude to Klee. This is a game that I love."

In the catalogue of his Robinson Crusoe exhibition, he admitted: "I am especially fond of things that I can steal, like books, pictures, scientific treatises, pieces of music, things I can approach by stealth: stealth in the sense of stealing. I have no problems about stealing. I steal with great pleasure and with no embarrassment."

That is Pericoli, the strolling player, the mountebank, the entertainer, which is also what he is.

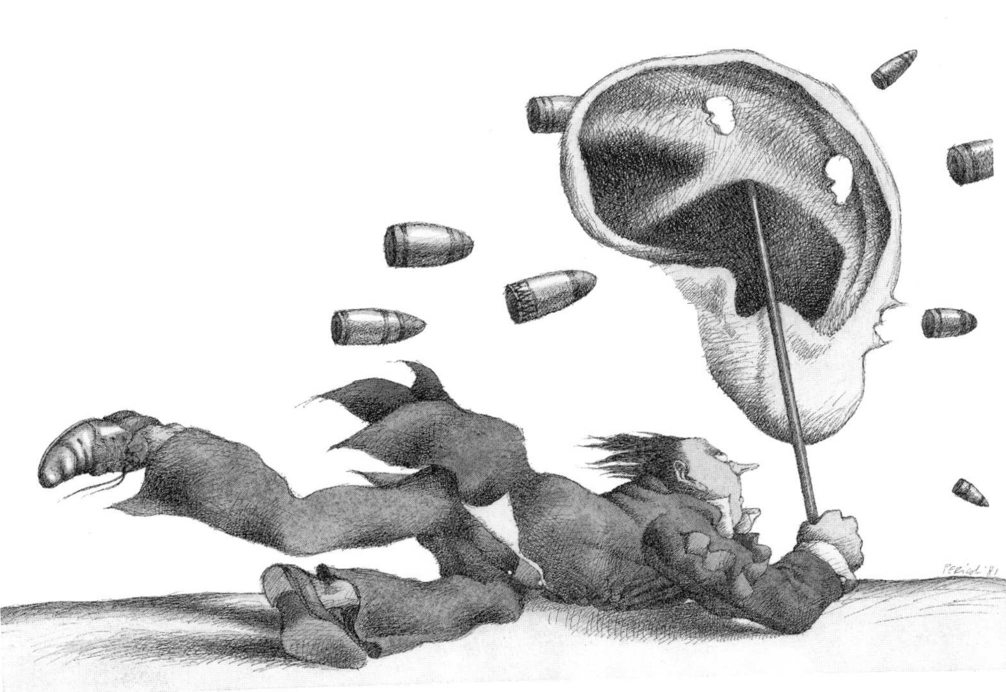

Fig. 19
The Big Ear, 1981
India ink and watercolor
on handmade card
38 x 57 cm (15 x 22.4 in.)

Certainly, his art involves collection and appropriation on a grand scale. The journalist collects the facts; the critic collects the truth behind all the lies and the pretense; the painter and draftsman collects everything that has ever been painted or drawn. He collects, accumulates, grabs; and still everything comes his way. He has it easy, but he also has it difficult. As a child of our century, he has everything within arm's reach, while being condemned to endure, day in and day out, an intolerable excess of outer and inner incidents. We sense how hard this must be. We marvel at the way he absorbs his people and the world itself. Pericoli's cool approach to the great is a salutary one for us. He does nothing to detract from their greatness – when they really are great – but he protects us from blind adulation and sharpens our own critical eye. For this our thanks are due to the clever, malicious, melancholy, mountebank of Milan: Tullio Pericoli, a man of many faces and many visions.

Georg Ramseger

Plates

Where no technique is specified,
all works are in india ink and watercolor
on handmade card

1

Greetings from Italy
1983

38 x 28.5 cm (15 x 11.2 in.)

2

David Levine

1987

50 x 38 cm (19.7 x 15 in.)

Pericoli '87

3

Literary Exercise

1984

38 x 28.5 cm (15 x 11.2 in.)

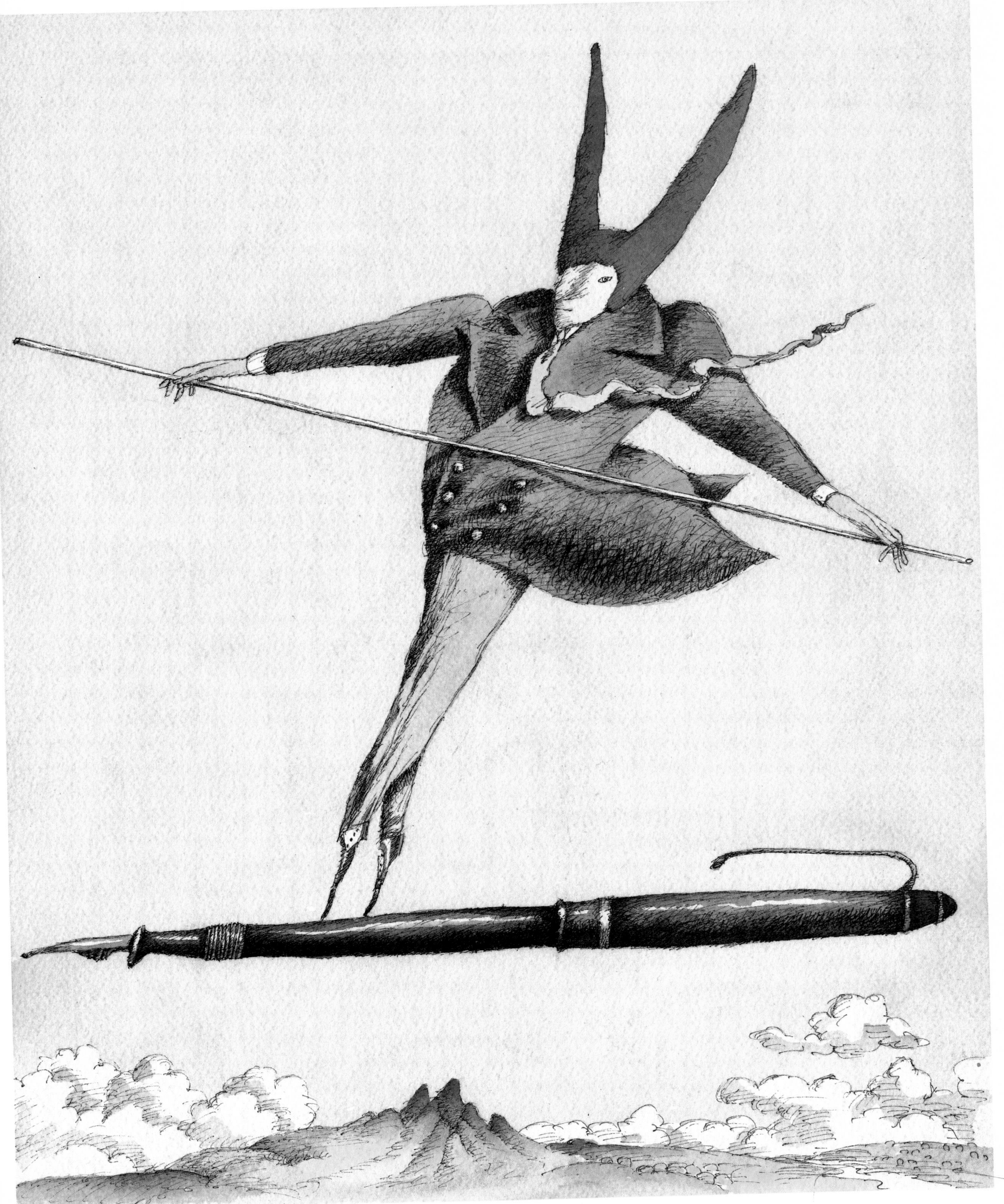

4

From A to Z

1986

57 x 38 cm (22.4 x 15 in.)

5

Italo Calvino

1987

57 x 38 cm (22.4 x 15 in.)

6

Ernest Hemingway
1986

38 x 57 cm (15 x 22.4 in.)

PERICOLI 86

7

Arthur Rimbaud

1987

57 x 38 cm (22.4 x 15 in.)

Pericoli '87

8

Franz Kafka

1986

57 x 38 cm (22.4 x 15 in.)

9

James Joyce
1987

61 x 38 cm (24 x 15 in.)

10

Samuel Beckett
1986

57 x 38 cm (22.4 x 15 in.)

11

Fyodor Dostoevsky
1980

38 x 55 cm (15 x 21.7 in.)

Pericoli 80

12

Eugenio Montale
1986

57 x 38 cm (22.4 x 15 in.)

Pericoli 86

13

Luigi Pirandello
1986

38 x 57 cm (15 x 22.4 in.)

14

Robert Louis Stevenson
1986

57 x 38 cm (22.4 x 15 in.)

15

Charles Baudelaire

1987

57 x 38 cm (22.4 x 15 in.)

16

Sigmund Freud
1986

57 x 38 cm (22.4 x 15 in.)

17

Albert Einstein

1987

57 x 38 cm (22.4 x 15 in.)

E=mc²
Zwiebeln 2,5
Orangen 3
Äpfel
Birnen
Trauben
Pericoli 87

18

Jean-Paul Sartre
1987

57 x 38 cm (22.4 x 15 in.)

SARTRE
Pericoli 87

19

Karl Raimund Popper
1987

57 x 38 cm (22.4 x 15 in.)

PERÍCOLI 87

20

Marcel Proust
1987

57 x 38 cm (22.4 x 15 in.)

21

Italo Svevo

1987

57 x 38 cm (22.4 x 15 in.)

PEricoli '87

22

Giacomo Leopardi
1987

38 x 44.5 cm (15 x 17.5 in.)

23

Günter Grass

1987

57 x 38 cm (22.4 x 15 in.)

Pericoli 87

24

Jacques Lacan
1987

57 x 38 cm (22.4 x 15 in.)

THE TOMB OF TUTANKH MEN
Israël
Le Nil
Erman. Hieroglyphen
EGYPTIAN READING BOOK
BUDGE
FIRST STEPS IN EGYPTIAN
BUDGE
CARL EINSTEIN-NEGERPLASTIK
Spiegelberg · Ägyptische
STEINDORFF · DIE KUNST DER ÄGYPTER
FECK-HEIMER
PLASTIK DER ÄGYPTER
Erman. Die ägyptische Religion
LES DEBUTS DE L'ART EN EGYPTE
PAR CAPART
A HISTORY OF EGYPT
PERICOLI
87

25

Benedetto Croce

1987

57 x 38 cm (22.4 x 15 in.)

26

Orson Welles
1987

57 x 38 cm (22.4 x 15 in.)

27

Milan Kundera

1987

57 x 38 cm (22.4 x 15 in.)

PERICOLI '87

28

Giorgio di Chirico
1986

57 x 38 cm (22.4 x 15 in.)

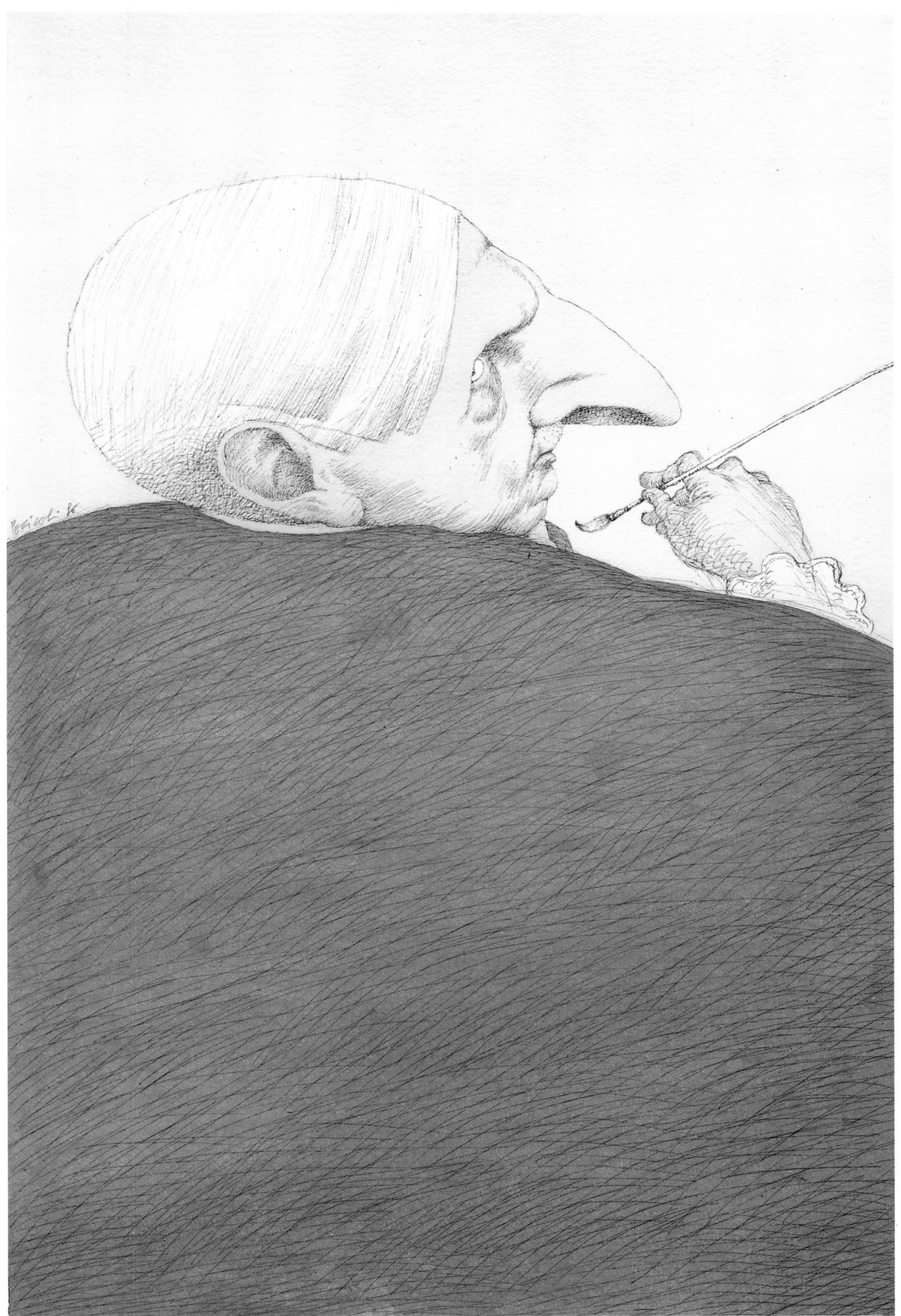

29

Virginia Woolf

1987

57 x 38 cm (22.4 x 15 in.)

Pericoli 87
ORLANDO
A BIOGRAPHY
THE HOGARTH PRESS
TO THE LIGHTHOUSE

30

Boris L. Pasternak
1987

57 x 38 cm (22.4 x 15 in.)

PERICOLI 87

31

Peter Handke

1987

57 x 38 cm (22.4 x 15 in.)

Pericoli 87

32

Jorge Luis Borges

1987

57 x 38 cm (22.4 x 15 in.)

PERÍCOLI 87

33

Robert Musil

1987

57 x 38 cm (22.4 x 15 in.)

34

Fernando Pessoa
1987

57 x 38 cm (22.4 x 15 in.)

35

Thomas Stearns Eliot

1987

57 x 38 cm (22.4 x 15 in.)

Pericoli 87

36

Primo Levi

1987

57 x 38 cm (22.4 x 15 in.)

Pericoli '87

37

Michel Foucault

1987

57 x 38 cm (22.4 x 15 in.)

38

Umberto Eco
1980

46 x 36.5 cm (18.1 x 14.4 in.)

PERICOLI 80

39

Figure in Space
1980

38 x 57 cm (15 x 22.4 in.)

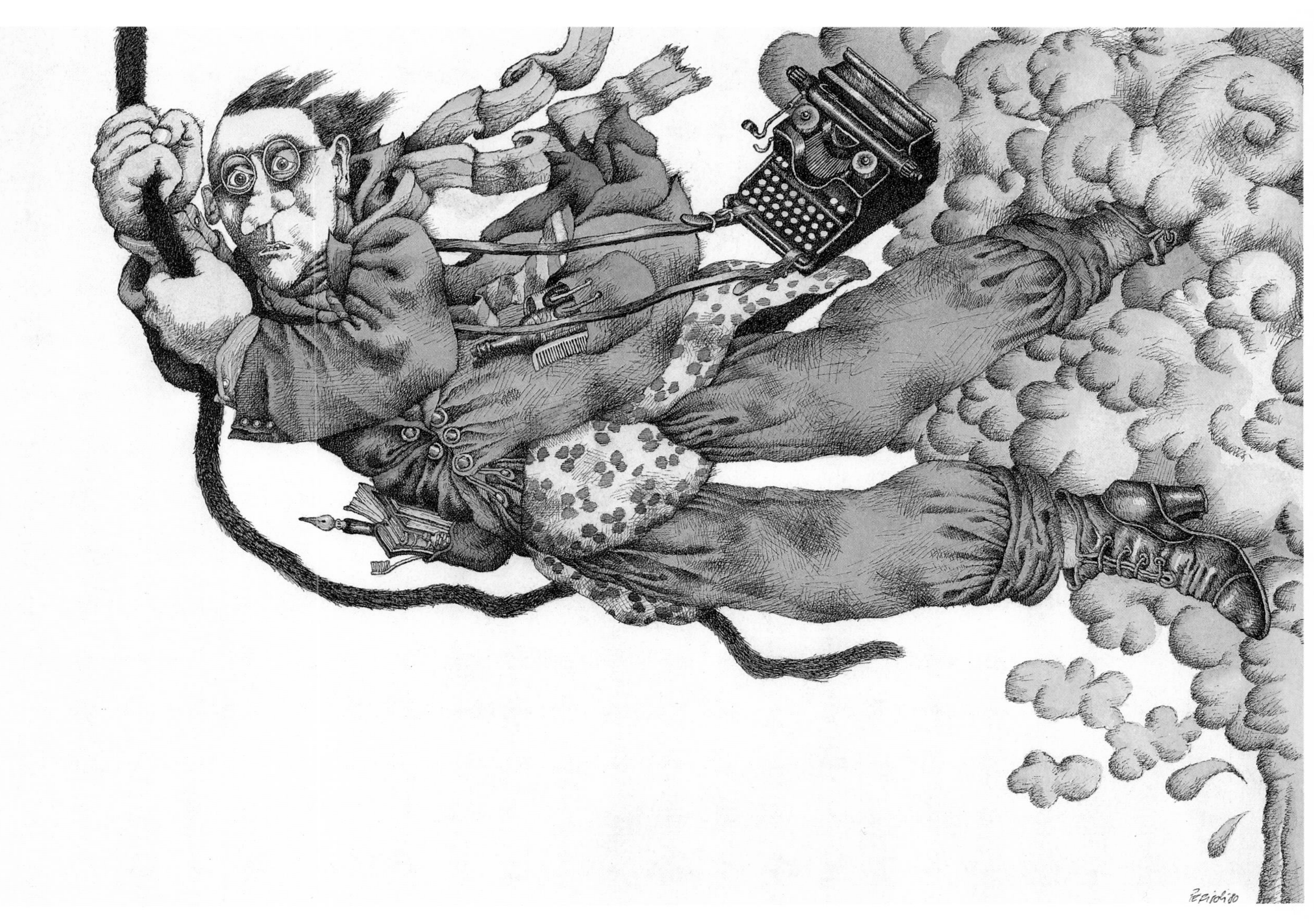

40

Comic Scene
1980

38 x 57 cm (15 x 22.4 in.)

41

Secondary Literature
1982

38 x 57 cm (15 x 22.4 in.)

42

Flying Leaves
1985

38 x 57 cm (15 x 22.4 in.)

PERICOLI

43

The Overview

1983

38 x 28.5 cm (15 x 11.2 in.)

44

On Film

1980

38 x 57 cm (15 x 22.4 in.)

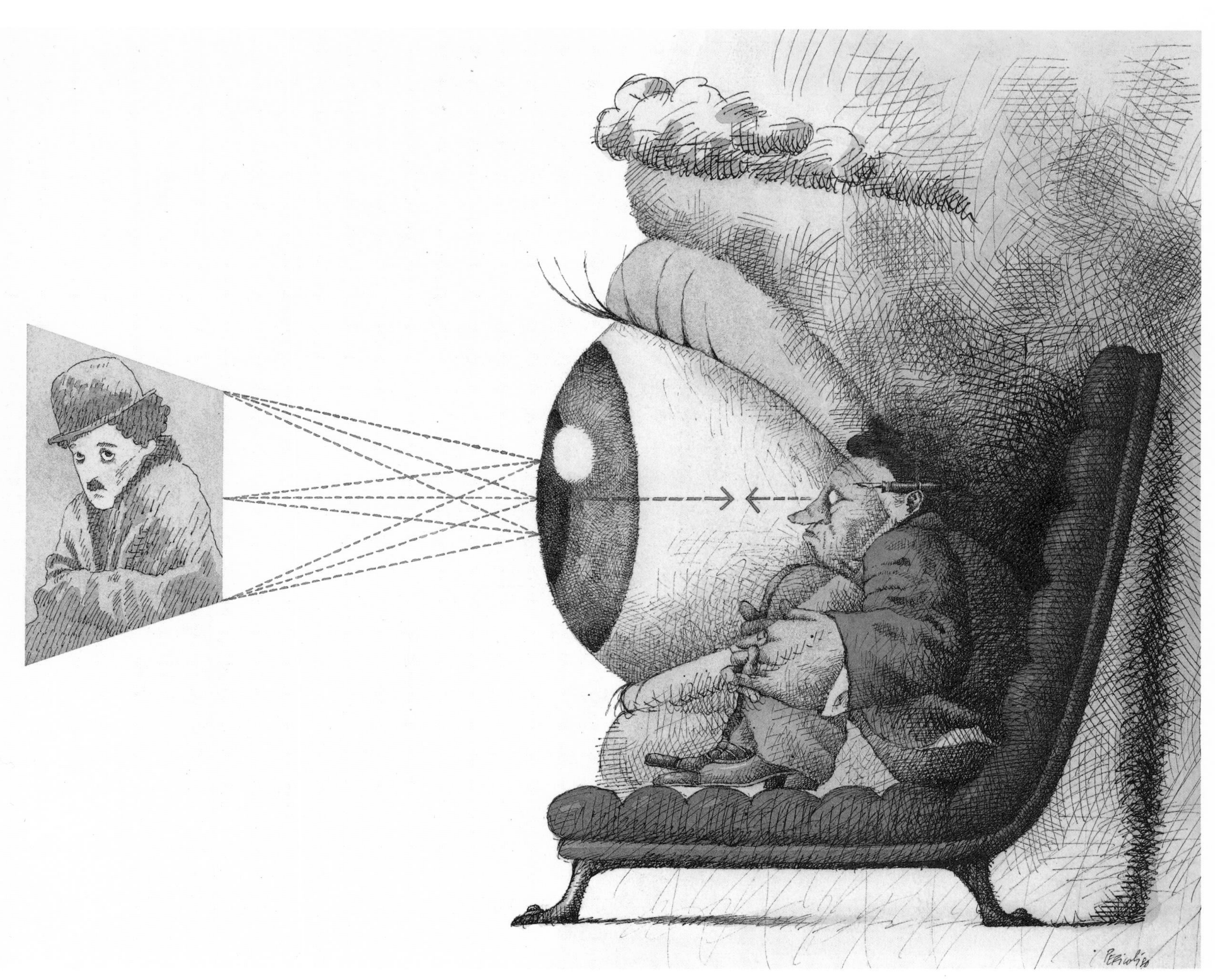

45

Luis Buñuel

1987

Pencil, watercolor, and pastel on paper

38 x 28.5 cm (15 x 11.2 in.)

Pericoli 87

46

Pier Paolo Pasolini
1986

57 x 38 cm (22.4 x 15 in.)

Pericoli 86

47

Woody Allen

1987

57 x 38 cm (22.4 x 15 in.)

Pericoli 87

48

Johann Sebastian Bach

1985

38 x 28.5 cm (15 x 11.2 in.)

1685
1985
Pericoli '85

49

Igor Stravinsky
1986

57 x 38 cm (22.4 x 15 in.)

50

Vladimir Horowitz
1986

57 x 38 cm (22.4 x 15 in.)

Pericoli 86

51

Charles Darwin
1986

57 x 38 cm (22.4 x 15 in.)

52

Mobile Thought

1985

38 x 28.5 cm (15 x 11.2 in.)

Pericoli

53

Milan: Piazza del Duomo

1982

57 x 38 cm (22.4 x 15 in.)

54

Beneath the Stars
1985

57 x 38 cm (22.4 x 15 in.)

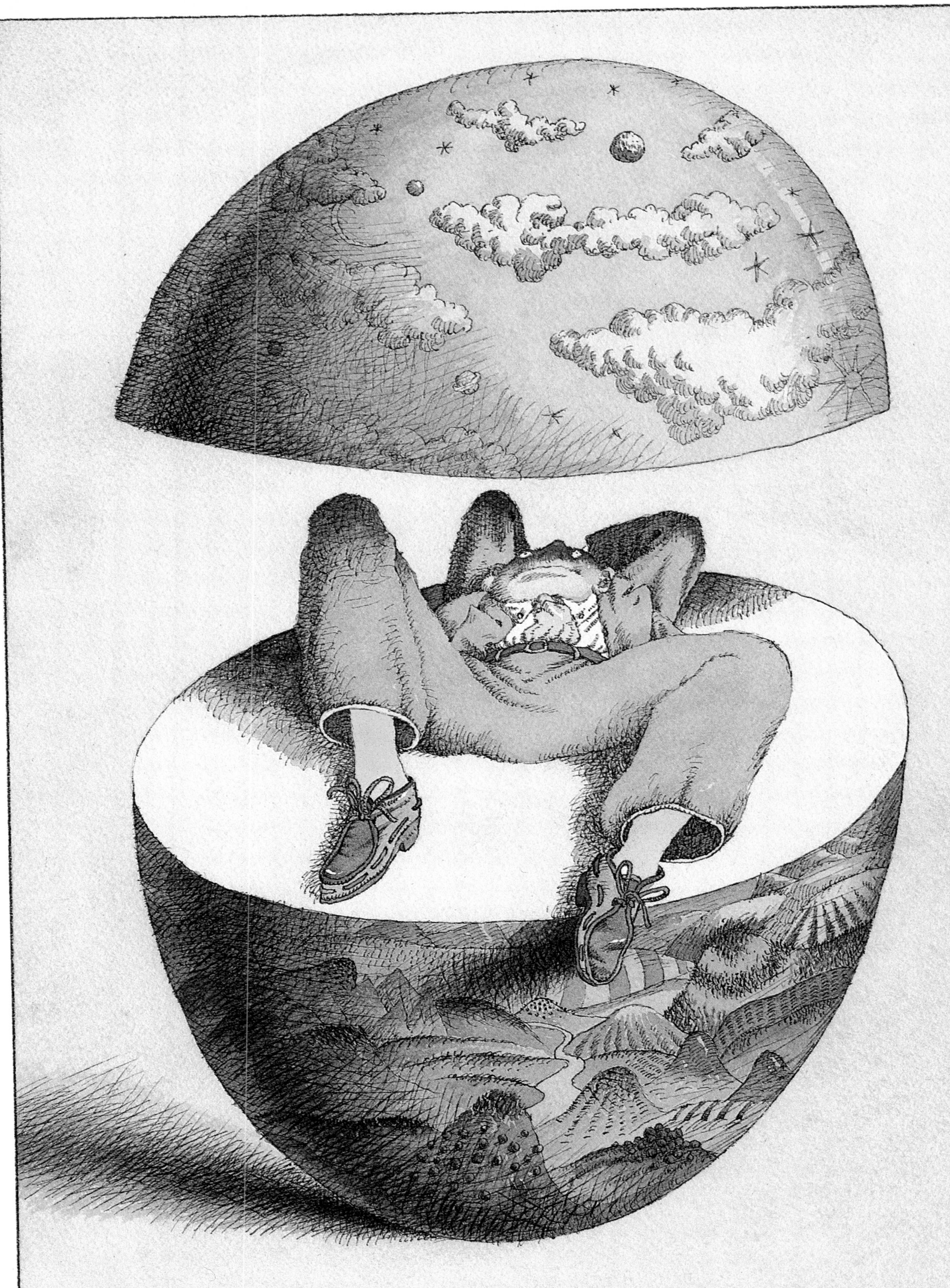
PERicoli

55

Composition

1985

57 x 38 cm (22.4 x 15 in.)

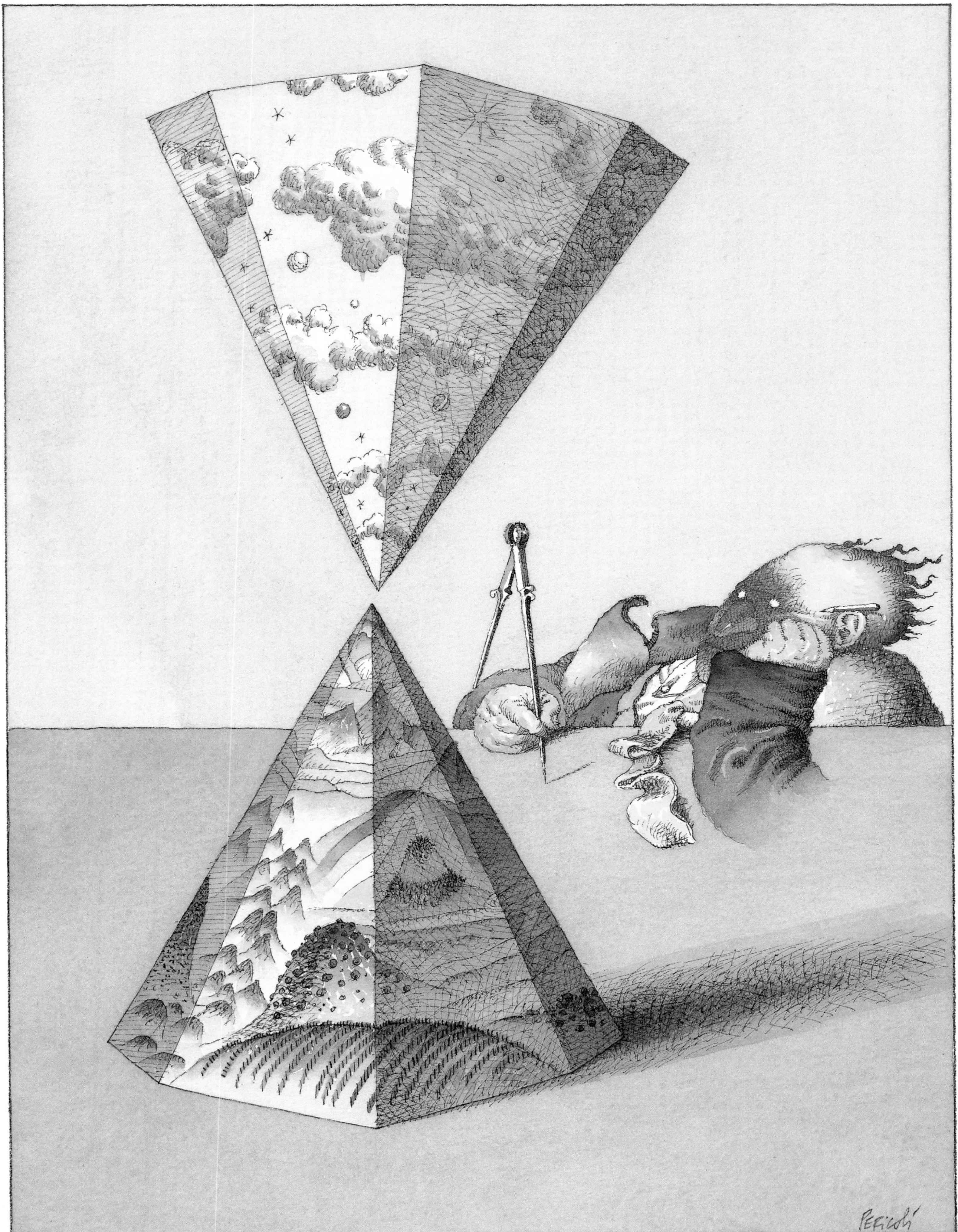

56

The Big A

1986

38 x 57 cm (15 x 22.4 in.)

PERicoli

57

Smoke in the Eyes
1986

38 x 57 cm (15 x 22.4 in.)

58

Cold Ball

1981

38 x 39 cm (15 x 15.4 in.)

PERICOLI '81

59

Unfinished Portrait

1985

38 x 28.5 cm (15 x 11.2 in.)

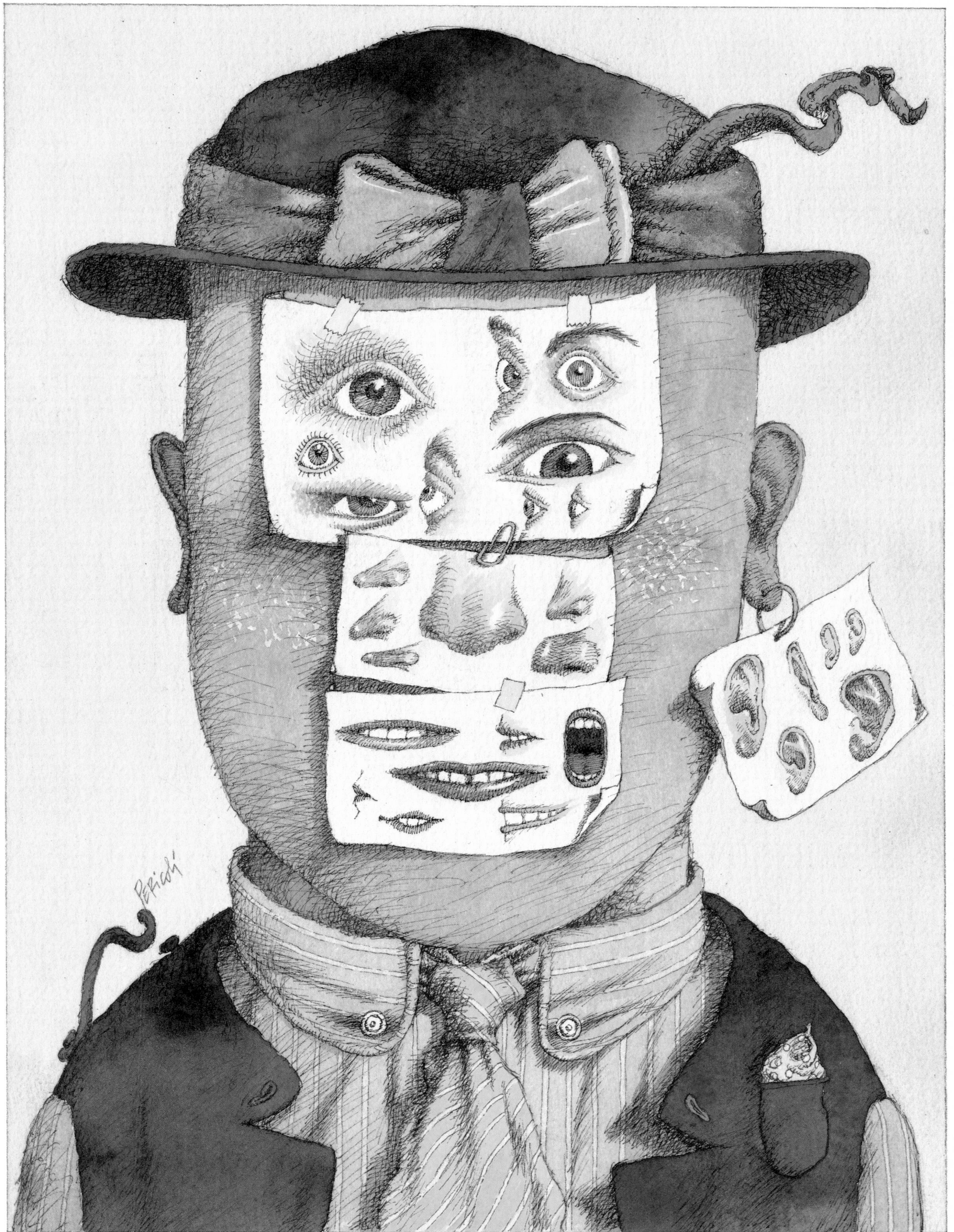
PERICOLI

Antonio Tabucchi

To Live or to Portray

"Today we're going to play at making a film," said the Artist. "Whatever you want, you can have. Let's pretend this is a film studio with a cameraman, a clapperboy, lighting technicians and set builders. Then imagine the actors waiting in the wings. The first thing we need of course is a director, but we can draw him too."

He took some paper and a brush and began drawing his film director; and to prevent the director feeling lonely he drew an Assistant on another sheet of paper, an intellectual-looking assistant whom he could talk to or argue with if he wanted. He drew an imposing, haughty director wearing a felt hat, his tie fluttering in the breeze from the electric fans. There was something disturbing about his face; this Artist did not enjoy games like board games that send you to sleep. He liked subversive games. He was convinced that real games, games that are worth playing, should alarm and not console. When he had finished he gave the director an encouraging pat on the back and said to him: "Now, Maestro, you can begin. Play's started. Clap!"

1.

The Maestro sat on the canvas director's chair, the one with Maestro written across the back. He was ready. By way of preparation he had transferred his left eye over his right one, concentrating both eyes into one in order to see better. He had encircled the double eye with the curled fingers of one hand so that everything he saw was inside a frame; he was accustomed to putting people into frames, in fact he was planning to frame everyone who was to appear before him that day: the actors in his new film. He called the clapperboy and the cameraman and told them he was ready. The clapperboy asked him what the film was called.

"What do you want a title for?" replied the Maestro.

The clapperboy explained that he needed to write it on his clapper board, so that he could say the title and then bang the clapper; to do his job properly he needed a title. The Maestro thought for a moment and then said without conviction: "Life is a Portrait."

"Portrait of Life would be preferable," protested the Assistant, who was sitting beside him.

"I lived by Portraying," retorted the Maestro.

"Living Portraits would be more appropriate," said the Assistant, "and more accurate too."

"Portraying to Live," said the Maestro in a tired voice. He seemed irritated already.

"To Live or to Portray," said the Assistent obstinately, "that's the correct title because that's the real question for artists like us. Nowadays we can't say if a portrait imitates life or if life imitates a portrait. And that is the tragedy of modern man. We are highly disorientated."

The Maestro silenced him with a gesture. "The second half is excellent," he said. "It's perfect." He turned to the clapperboy and said decisively: "Or to Portray. That is the definitive title."

The clapperboy wrote OR TO PORTRAY on the little blackboard of the clapperboard. Then he picked up the clapperboard with two hands, opened its jaws and shouted: "Or to Portray! Take one! James!" And he banged the clapper energetically.

2.

The first actor arrived and looked about him in bewilderment. He was thin, with a small moustache, spectacles and a walking stick. He was very elegantly dressed, with a waistcoat and bow tie, though his beautiful red jacket was showing signs

60

Federico Fellini
1985

38 x 57 cm (15 x 22.4 in.)

of wear at the elbows. The Maestro signed to him to come forward, and he advanced with uncertain steps. He used his stick with elegance and ease, as if he were out for a stroll, but on closer observation it became clear that he was testing the ground with it, feeling his way. He must only be able to see us very dimly. Then he stumbled painfully, but managed to regain his dignity and reached the bookshelves on the wall without falling. He leant his stick against the shelves, slipped a book off the shelf, opened it and, arranging his feet like a tightrope walker, propped one elbow on the walking stick. It was obvious that he had learned his part to perfection. He watched for the Maestro's approval, and the Maestro winked his double eye affirmatively. The actor pulled a magnifying glass out of his pocket and brought it close to the printed page. Then he stood, waiting for instructions, eyeing the Maestro again.

"The whole of yourself is in that book," said the Maestro, "do you understand? I'd like you to get back into that book, if possible."

The actor looked at him quizzically, and did not move.

"Your childhood in Ireland," the Maestro continued, "your old folk, your priests, your dead. Get back into the circle again."

The actor looked at him in amazement and gave no hint of having understood. So the Maestro began to speak slowly and clearly, as if he were reciting a nursery rhyme or a lullaby. His voice was smooth and persuasive, and while he spoke the actor closed his eyes, as if a spell had been cast over him.

"And your woman as well," murmured the Maestro, "*the* woman, the essence of womanhood, that part of woman which is the most womanly: your Molly, the way in to the Universe."

The actor began to twist and turn as if someone were tickling his back. Then he crossed his legs and, with the hand that was holding the book, felt his trousers. "Can you see anything?" he asked nervously, looking down. Fortunately he was wearing baggy trousers, and nothing was visible. The Maestro shook his head and gave a little sign of

Study for *James Joyce*, 1987
Pencil on paper
35 x 28 cm (13.8 x 11 in.)

encouragement. The actor dived into his book again, bent his head, bent his shoulders in an effort to get back into the book that was his whole self. His body spiralled round, turning endlessly around itself. The Maestro nodded agreement to his assistants and the cameraman shouted: "Hold it a minute! Perfect!"

3.

"Or to Portray! Benedetto!" shouted the clapperboy. And he banged the clapper energetically.

Another actor appeared. An old man looking very annoyed, and glancing about him suspiciously.

"I'd like to make it clear that I'm an amateur actor," he said to the Maestro, who was watching him. Then, turning to the Assistant, he enunciated: "am – a – teur." His voice was full of sarcasm, but the Assistant did not react. Anyway, it would be hard to say exactly what was so provocative in his bearing. Perhaps it was just his way of speaking, or the way he dragged his feet as he came slowly on to the stage. The Maestro and the Assistant noticed he was wearing slippers on his feet. He noticed that they had noticed and, still looking

He noticed that they had noticed and, still looking as if there were a bad smell under his nose, he said hastily: "Your agent, or impresario or whatever, came to collect me when I was having my afternoon nap. I didn't even have time to put my shoes on." Then he explained: "I *always* have a nap in the afternoon."

He spoke as if everyone else were to blame. That was why he seemed so provocative: he provoked an uneasy feeling of guilt. As if exhausted, he reached the table in the middle of the stage and asked: "Well, what shall I do?" He looked round and added: "This place is a mess. Everything ought to be put tidily away in its proper place."

The Maestro told him to sit down at the table, and he sat down.

"I don't understand why you came for me, rather than anyone else. What part do you want me to play?"

"Oh, no one in particular," said the Maestro. "Your face reminded me of someone, and I'm looking for a certain expression which I thought perhaps you could reproduce." After a short pause he added: "And I wanted you to see my film studio, and to see the way I make instant portraits."

The old man opened his eyes in surprise, looking even more disgusted than before.

"It's an art form," explained the Maestro patiently.

"Art is art," mumbled the old man through his teeth, "and it doesn't manifest itself in rubbish like this, young man. This is the way it has always been, and this is the way it always will be. My wife agrees with me." He had propped his face on one hand and assumed a defensive expression like someone waiting to see which way the argument will go.

"What do you mean by art?" the Maestro asked politely.

The old man coughed and spat on the floor. "Um...," he mumbled, "um... I mean... poetry, of course. Because that's the way it is, young man; either it's poetry or it's not poetry, there's no getting away from that."

"I'm trying to create a tableau vivant," said the Maestro, "I don't know if I make myself clear."

The old man grew pale with disgust. His face took on a profoundly sceptical look; he seemed tired, terribly tired.

"Bohemianism," he said with revulsion, "modernism." And his lower lip, damp and soft, dropped.

The Maestro framed him with his double eye, adjusted the focus and signed to the cameraman to zoom in for a close up of just his face. The cameraman got the message at once and shouted: "Hold it a moment! Perfect!"

4.

"Or to Portray! Fyodor!" shouted the clapperboy. And banged the clapper energetically.

"You really are a master, Maestro," whispered the Assistant admiringly, taking advantage of the late arrival of the next player. Then he began taking notes frantically.

The door opened a crack and two voices shouted in unison: "There are two of us! We're the Terrible Twins!"

"Your names?" asked the Maestro.

"Smith and Jones!" shouted the two voices, in unison.

"Just one moment," commanded the Maestro, "you must come in by the other door." Then he turned to the set builder and whispered: "Make them come in by the Duchamp door."

The set builder disappeared behind the scenes and his footsteps could be heard crossing the stage. The Maestro picked up the megaphone and asked them to make an entrance through the doorways at right angles to each other, requesting that the one called first should make his entrance first. He signed to the cameraman to be ready and said: "When I lower my hand please call Smith to come forward." He lowered his hand,and at the same moment called: "Come forward, Jones!" The Assistant looked at him astonished, and the Maestro whispered perfidiously: "You have to use duplicity with doubles."

"Hold it a moment! Perfect!" shouted the cameraman.

But he had no need to say it because the Terrible Twins were standing motionless in the Duchamp door, wearing the perplexed and mortified look of people who know they have been tricked.

5.

"Or to Portray! Franz!" shouted the clapperboy, and banged his clapper energetically.

An emaciated young man with prominent cheek bones and large, flapping ears came in. He was wearing a black overcoat and a black hat and looked somewhat lugubrious. The stage was dark, and a spotlight bathed the young man in a greenish light.

"I was summoned a year ago, and I still haven't understood why," said the young man. "In the note it said that the Maestro wanted to speak to me. I don't know who the Maestro is or why he wants to see me. I'd like to know what I'm being accused of, at least."

"No one is accusing you of anything," said the Maestro calmly. "For the time being."

This "for the time being" seemed to alarm the actor, who said irrelevantly: "Last night I stopped at an inn, where I had dinner and slept. I made the acquaintance of a waitress, and we chatted about this and that. I'm tired of this job, it doesn't lead anywhere."

The Assistant looked at the script on his knee and shuddered with indignation. These were not his lines. Just as with the preceding actors, someone, unknown to him, had changed the script, twisting it around arbitrarily, introducing whole new sentences. Or perhaps the actors were improvising. The latter theory calmed him down for a moment, even though he knew it could not be true, because certain lines cannot be improvised.

"I'm tired of this job. It doesn't lead to anything." And in response to signs from the Maestro he moved across the stage. When he got to the photographs he stopped, and the spotlights on the right lit up, bathing the stage in a spectral glow. The dark silhouette of the actor was sharply etched against the white background of the screen.

"Do you like those photographs?" enquired the Maestro.

The actor looked at them tenderly, proudly. "I was charming," he said, with a mocking sneer on his face. "I, I, I, I . . . and him." He opened his coat and closed it again.

"You detest real, flesh and blood people," said the Maestro irrelevantly. "You're frightened of them. They fill you with envy and contempt."

The actor was reassured. "Blood," he said, "that horrible fluid that governs our lives." Then he flapped the wings of his overcoat and stood on tiptoe, as if about to fly away. The Maestro made a sign to the cameraman.

"Hold it a moment! Perfect!" shouted the cameraman.

6.

"Or to Portray! Sigmund!" shouted the clapperboy. And he banged the clapper energetically.

The actor turned round calmly and surveyed them from behind his little round spectacles. He had been on the stage for a long time, but had not been spotlighted until now.

"He will come to the end of the skein," he said in a tone of voice that admitted no rejoinder. "Whoever gave me this fishing rod must have been mad; and he must also have thought you have to go down to the water to fish. The fact is that any old ditch will do, because what matters is not what you catch but the way you catch it. That is the strength of the true novelists. I mean, it's the bait that counts. If there are any fish they will take the bait."

"Tell me about yourself," said the Maestro.

"About myself?!" exclaimed the old actor. "It would be more appropriate if you told me about yourself, my dear chap, and then I would give you my opinion." And he looked at the Maestro as if he were a microbe.

The cameraman shouted: "Hold it a moment! Perfect!"

7.

"Or to Portray! Italo!" shouted the clapperboy. And he banged the clapper energetically.

"What's this hole?" asked the actor, peering out of the hole.

"Just a hole," replied the Maestro kindly.

"And... I beg your pardon. Was I brought here just to peer out of a hole?"

"If you would be so good," said the Maestro.

"If I've understood you correctly, you've made me cut my hair like a brush, lose weight, grow a moustache and wear a cigarette stuck behind my ear like a barber – all of this so that I can peer through a hole?"

"If you would be so good," said the Maestro.

The actor twisted his neck and had a look at the canvas he was peering out of. It was a painted back-cloth, like the back-cloths they have at fairs; you put your head through a hole in the middle to be photographed and you are transformed into Tarzan, King Kong, or the Red Baron in his airplane. He looked at the female face painted next to his and exclaimed in surprise: "Good heavens, that's my wife!" He opened his eyes wide with glee and said, "Oh, ho, my darling little wife, arm in arm with her little husband," and giggled satirically.

The Maestro was watching the situation attentively. By now, however, the scene was well under way and the actor was playing his part to perfection.

"For someone like me there's nothing better than pretending to be myself," he said. "I do it every day. Look, Maestro, now I take my little wife on my arm and we go for a stroll down the Corso. I'm a proud husband, a solemn, respectable husband... these fairground backdrops are so solemn and respectable. Take a look, Maestro. My marriage, my life – they are all in the raising of my eyebrow."

The Maestro made a sign to the cameraman, and the cameraman shouted; "Hold it a moment! Perfect!"

Study for
Italo Svevo, 1987
India ink and
pastel
on paper
35 x 28 cm
(13.8 x 11 in.)

8.

"So sorry, but I won't have a screen test," he said, before the clapperboy had time to shout; he was a man with a moustache and a hat who emerged from behind three motionless figures, all looking exactly like him. "I've already had all the tests, played all the parts."

Everyone looked at him, amazed. The Maestro's double eye widened in surprise. The man with the moustache and the hat was unperturbed. "My dear Maestro, you want to make me act on this stage, but I'm afraid that your laudable efforts would be to little avail. My own soul is the theater of my emotions."

The Maestro managed to get over his surprise and picked up the megaphone.

"Tell him to stop!" he shouted to his assistants. The man interrupted him with a gesture – but so imperious a gesture that nobody moved. He went up to the stage and said: "I could not exactly say if this is a melodrama or a comedy. My author is reticent on this matter, and that's my tragedy. I live between the two as if they were one, and the one is neither one nor the other. My screen test would be a disaster, that's one thing I'm sure of at least."

"I don't know what you're driving at," said the Maestro.

The man sneezed; an obviously fake sneeze, exaggerated, as if to cover something else. "I implore you," he murmured, "don't ask me direct questions, don't challenge my sense of irony."

"I don't know what you're driving at," said the Maestro, in his voice that admits no rejoinder.

"To expose your contemptible tricks," replied the man, as if accepting the challenge.

"I don't know how you would be able to do that," said the Maestro.

The man took the pen from his pocket, went up to the white canvas that was just behind him and, with a speed at variance with his previous leisurely pace, drew an enormous finger print composed entirely of illegible words.

"That's my portrait," he said, "it's a present for you." Then he bowed slightly and, placing his hand on his heart, made the following speech in an exaggeratedly histrionic voice: "Here I am. I'm Pessoa, and they told me to be like this; let's say that I'm an actor and that I've come to entertain you, or, if you prefer, let's say that I'm Pessoa who for this evening is pretending to be an actor impersonating Fernando Pessoa."

He stood motionless. The cameraman released the shutter, and the Maestro clapped warmly. "Perfect," he shouted, "perfect!"

It was only now that the Assistant understood what had happened. Dazed, he looked at the Maestro and said: "You agreed?"

"Of course," the Maestro replied with satisfaction.

9.

"And now let's take a break," said the Maestro to the Assistant. "Or rather, let's take a little look at the future. I've still got a long queue of players to dream up, but first I'd like to tell you about the character who is to appear at the close of the film. I shall need your collaboration."

"What can I do for you?" asked the Assistant.

Study for *Fernando Pessoa*, 1987
India ink and pastel on paper,
35 x 28 cm (13.8 x 11 in.)

"Oh, it's very simple," said the Maestro. "I've got to portray someone whose face I don't know. So I'd like you to stand in for him."

"If that's all it is," said the Assistant, "it seems very straightforward." And he climbed onto the stage. The curtain rose and revealed a bed. Under the bed could be seen a chaotic mess of paint brushes, pencils, drawings, books, tubes of paint.

"Put on the nightshirt and get into bed," the Maestro ordered. The Assistant accomplished that task and then he asked what he should do next.

"Open your eyes wide as if you had just woken up," said the Maestro. "You are the Artist and you've woken up from the dream in which you were drawing us all."

"I'm afraid I don't understand," said the Assistant.

"Our Artist," said the Maestro, "who is drawing us all."

The Assistant looked at him with staring eyes.

"But what are you saying, Maestro?" he said with a note of panic in his voice.

"I want to do a portrait of the person who has done my portrait," said the Maestro, and his voice sounded hardly human.

And then, as the pupil of his double eye shrank to the size of a pin prick, he said: "I am a portrait!"

The Assistant pulled off the bedclothes and sat on the bed.

"And so are you," said the Maestro menacingly. "Hold it a moment!"

The Assistant jumped out of bed and began to back away, covering his face with his hands. He stumbled. He fell. He got up again. "I don't want to," he shouted. "I'm real... I exist." He threaded his way past the scenery and began to run. As he ran he passed all the characters who were waiting for their screen tests; when they saw him in such an extraordinary state they laughed mockingly at him. "I don't want to become a portrait," he shouted, running away through the theater. "Help! Help!"

10.

"Help! Help!" shouted the Artist, and woke up. His forehead was glistening with sweat. He sat up in bed and said: "Hell! What a strange dream. I dreamed that as a joke I drew a Maestro who could draw portraits; using his Assistant as a pretext he wanted to turn me into a portrait as well."

He turned on the light on the bedside table and tried to regain his sense of reality. Before going to sleep he had left his room in a great mess, and this added to his sense of disorientation. He looked at himself in the mirror in front of him and noticed that he looked extremely disturbed, like someone waking from an exceptionally bizarre dream. He stared fixedly at his face in the glass, and just then his reflection opened its mouth and said: "Hold it a moment! Perfect!"

Appendix

Chronology

Photo: Armin Linke

1936–1960 Born at Colli del Tronto (in the province of Ascoli Piceno), a tiny village in the Marches, Tullio Pericoli attends high school in Ascoli Piceno. He spends his free afternoons on copying old masters in the town's art museum, the Pinacoteca, in the hope that his talent will be discovered. He succeeds, even if not by this means, in obtaining private drawing lessons from the director of the Pinacoteca, the painter Ernesto Ercolani.

In his last years at school he helps a friend to boost sales of the local daily newspaper: Pericoli's caricatures of local dignitaries appear in the paper every day. After graduating from high school, Pericoli studies law in Rome and Urbino. He is already earning his living by supplying drawings and illustrations to various papers.

1961 Pericoli abandons his studies, shortly before the examination, and moves to Milan. Over the next ten years he works for the daily paper *Il Giorno*, which regularly publishes his cartoons and illustrations in its arts pages. He also draws for other papers and magazines, and develops a reputation not only as an illustrator but as a painter.

1972 The Institute of Art History at Parma University mounts a large exhibition of Pericoli's paintings.

In the same year he embarks on a fruitful association with the magazine *Linus*, which popularizes American comics of high quality in Italy. Working with his friend Emanuele Pirella, he publishes satirical and political cartoons – a genre practically extinct in Italy since World War II, which Pericoli and Pirella succeed in reviving by their committed advocacy.

1974 A contract with the newspaper *Corriere della sera* gives Pericoli a regular arts-page outlet for illustrations, cartoons, and drawings.

1976 Again with Pirella, he creates for *Corriere della sera* the series "Tutti da Fulvia sabato sera," in which, every Saturday, he passes satirical comment on Italian cultural life.

Pericoli begins to draw regularly for the weekly news magazine *L'Espresso*. The contract with *Corriere della sera* comes to an end.

Pericoli's paintings go on show at the Studio Marconi gallery, in Milan. Over the next ten years, Studio Marconi will present a number of exhibitions of his paintings.

Pericoli is introduced to the German public by the advertising design magazine, *novum*.

1978 Parma University mounts an exhibition of cartoons, comic strips, and political caricatures. Urbino University mounts an exhibition on the theme of "Drawing (as a free art) & Drawing (as a means of communication in the most varied media)."

1979 Exhibitions in Genoa, Milan, and Rome; Olivetti presents a large exhibition of paintings in Ivrea.

1980 *Rubare a Klee* ("Stealing from Klee") is the title of a one-man show at Galleria del Milione in Milan, in which Pericoli sets out the secret of his pictorial invention. His analyses and his studies all center on the work of Paul Klee. In a dialogue between Pericoli and Italo Calvino, published on the occasion of the exhibition, both men stress the necessity of having artistic models and define themselves, in their own respective fields, as "thieves" – stealers of words, of motifs, and of techniques.

1981 The committee of the Venice Biennale organizes with Pericoli an exhibition on the theme of the consumption of culture by the media.

Pericoli takes part in an exhibition on modern television production design at the Milan Triennale.

1983 On behalf of the Olivetti company, the writer Giorgio Soavi commissions Pericoli to illustrate a book of his choice. Pericoli chooses *Robinson Crusoe*. This is a theme that allows him to resolve, to his own satisfaction, the constant conflict between his task as a painter and as an illustrator and draftsman. Painting and drawing, landscape and face/figure, blend into the unified work of a single artist.

1984 Pericoli starts working for the daily paper *La Repubblica*, where, with Pirella, he revives "Fulvia." The collaboration continues to the present day.

The Olivetti presentation volume, *Robinson Crusoe*, is published.

"Alberto Moravia, you have just married at the age of seventy-eight."
"Yes."
"What place does eroticism occupy in your life?"
"The same as when I was twenty."
"So are you marrying for the sake of sensuality or sexuality?"
"For love."
"But can there be love without sex?"
"There can be sex without love, but not love without sex."
"Let's go on to some more general questions. – Do you prefer to do it standing up or lying down?"

From the series "Saturday Night at Fulvia's," *La Repubblica*, January 19, 1986

The Swiss periodical *graphis* publishes an article on Pericoli, with special reference to his *Robinson Crusoe* illustrations. As a result, he is contacted by a Munich gallery, Bartsch & Chariau.

1985 The exhibition *Disegni per Robinson, paesaggi e personaggi* is held at the Padiglione d'Arte Contemporanea, Milan. The same exhibition travels to Bologna and Genoa in 1986, and to Rome University in 1987.

Pericoli's association with Studio Marconi ends.

New drawings: subtly worked out satirical portraits of writers, scientists, artists, and philosophers. Starts contributing portraits of writers to the literary magazine *L'Indice*.

First exhibition in Germany: portraits and drawings at Galerie Bartsch & Chariau, Munich. This leads to the idea of another exhibition at the Wilhelm-Busch-Museum, Hanover, and of a book in Germany.

1986 The magazine *grafik – visuelles marketing* publishes an article on the Munich exhibition.

Pericoli confronts a new challenge when he is comissioned by Italian television to design logos for specific programmes.

1987 The complete portraits for *L'Indice* tour northern Italy in a touring exhibition.

The Munich firm of Hanser-Verlag publishes a short-story series, *Hansers Bibliothek der Erzähler*, with cover motifs by Pericoli.

At the end of the year Pericoli resigns from *L'Espresso*.

1988 Publication of the German edition of this book, *Woody, Freud und andere*, in conjunction with a showing of the artist's work at the Wilhelm-Busch-Museum, Hanover; the Westfälisches Landesmuseum, Münster; the Stadt- und Schiffahrtsmuseum, Kiel (1989); and the Museum für Kunst und Gewerbe, Hamburg (1989).

Pericoli paints a mural for Italian publisher Garzanti.

1989 Start of cooperation with the *Frankfurter Allgemeine Zeitung* (literary section every Saturday).

Exhibition in the Museumspavillion, municipal gallery, Salzburg.

Principal exhibitions

C–*collective exhibition* I–*individual exhibition*

1964 Galleria del Teatro, Parma (I)

1967 Galleria Gianferrati, Milan (I)

1971 Galleria dello Scudo, Verona (I)

1972 Salone dei Contraforti in Pilotta, organized by Istituto di Storia dell'Arte, Parma University (I)

1974 Libreria Einaudi, Milan (I)

1976 Galleria Solferino, Milan (I)

La cosa disegnata, Studio Marconi, Milan (I)

Galleria Facchetti, Zürich (G)

Galleria Rondanini, Rome (I)

1977 Sala comunale d'arte contemporanea, Alessandria (I)

La traccia del racconto, Villa comunale Ormond, San Remo (C)

1978 Galleria la Chiocciola, Padua (I)

Scuderia in Pilotta, organized by Centro Studi and Archivio della Comunicazione, Parma University (I)

Disegno e disegno, Urbino University (I)

Galleria La Nuova Città, Brescia (I)

Studio Marconi, Milan (I)

La Parola, Modigliana (C)

Artisti in Lombardia negli anni sessanta, Munich (C)

1979 Servizi culturali Olivetti, Ivrea (I)

Ars combinatoria, Galleria d'Arte moderna, Bologna; Teatro Falcone, Genoa (C)

Testuale – Le parole e le immagini, Rotonda di via Besana, Milan (C)

Le torri dipinte, Galleria Il Segno, Rome (I)

1980 Galleria Il Sole, Bolzano (I)

Rubare a Klee, Galleria del Milione, Milan (I)

1981 *Lombardia, vent'anni dopo*, Castello Visconteo, Pavia (I)

Galleria la Chiocciola, Padua (C)

Il consumo culturale, Biennale di Venezia, Venice (C)

La frase e il discorso, Cortina d'Ampezzo (C)

Lo spazio scenografico della TV italiana, XVI Triennale, Milan (C)

Segni d'acqua, Moderna Museet, Södertälje, Sweden (C)

1982 *Scrittura attiva*, Galleria d'Arte contemporanea, Suzzara (C)

Paesaggio italiano, Studio Marconi, Milan (I)

Paesaggio italiano e altri paesaggi, Palazzina dei Giardini pubblici, Assessorato alla Cultura, Modena (I)

1984 *Paesaggio*, Galleria Il Segno, Roma (I)

1985 *Arte cotta*, Studio Marconi, Milan (C)

Disegni per Robinson, paesaggio e personaggi, Padiglione d'Arte contemporanea (PAC), Milan; Galleria d'Arte moderna, Bologna; Museo Villa Croce, Genoa (I)

Dieci grafici per Napoli, Museo Aragona Pignatelli Cortes, Naples (C)

Galerie Bartsch & Chariau, Munich (I)

1986 *Fabula*, Studio Arte Nazzari, Parma; Galleria Tommaseo, Trieste; Galleria Cinquetti, Verona (C)

Le copertine di Repubblica, Galleria Il Segno, Rome (I)

Disegni per Robinson, Università "La Sapienza," Rome (I)

1987 *Quarantanove ritratti*, Civic Pinacoteca, Ascoli Piceno; Trento; Turin (I)

1988 *Quarantanove ritratti*, Istituto italiano di cultura, Lisbon (I)

Wilhelm-Busch-Museum, Hanover; Westfälisches Landesmuseum, Münster (I)

1989 Stadt- und Schiffahrtsmuseum, Kiel; Museum für Kunst und Gewerbe, Hamburg (I)

Selected Publications

Books by Tullio Pericoli

Contessa che è mai la vita, Milan 1970

Identikit di illustri sconosciuti, Milan 1974 (with Emanuele Pirella)

Il centro sinistra biodegradato, Florence 1975 (with Emanuele Pirella)

Fogli di vita, Turin 1976

I mostri descritti da Pintor e disegnati da Pericoli, Rome 1976

Il dottor Rigolo, Milan 1976 (with Emanuele Pirella)

Tutti da Fulvia sabato sera, Milan 1978 (with Emanuele Pirella)

Cronache di Palazzo, Milan 1979 (with Emanuele Pirella)

Le gioie dell'occhio, Milan 1981

Falsetto, Milan 1982 (with Emanuele Pirella)

Tutti da Fulvia, Milan 1987 (with Emanuele Pirella)

Book illustrations

Daniel Defoe, *Robinson Crusoe*, Olivetti, Milan 1984

Catalogues

Tullio Pericoli, geologie dell'io, Istituto di Storia dell'Arte, Università di Parma, 1972

Pericoli-Pirella, Centro di Studi e Archivio della Comunicazione, Università di Parma, Milan 1978

Furti ad arte: Italo Calvino e Tullio Pericoli, Edizioni della Galleria Il Milione, Milan 1980

Tullio Pericoli, Paesaggio italiano, text by Giulio Carlo Argan, Studio Marconi, Milan 1982

Tullio Pericoli, Disegni per Robinson, paesaggi e personaggi, texts by Umberto Eco, Tullio Pericoli, Francesco Poli, Milan 1985

Tullio Pericoli, Le copertine di Repubblica, Galleria Il Segno, Rome 1986

Tullio Pericoli, Quarantanove ritratti, texts by Francesco Poli, Enrico Castelnuovo, *L'Indice*, 1987